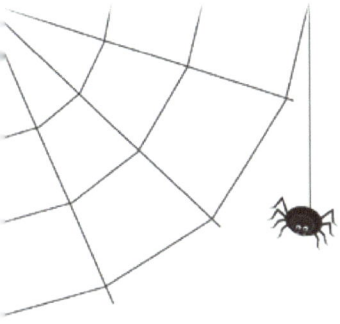

Halloween at Samson Parker's House

Samson Parker Books

Book 2

MJ Parker

ISBN: 0692856846
ISBN 13: 9780692856840
Library of Congress Control Number: 2017937759
LCCN Imprint Name: Rottweiler Tales Publishing, Plainsboro, NJ

Preface

This is the second book in a series written for children, although anyone can read them. Rottweiler Tales offers true stories about Samson Parker, who just happens to be a Rottweiler. We hope the series will educate people and let them know that Rottweilers are loyal, amazing dogs who, when raised with the right family, are the best dogs anyone could hope to have.

This book is dedicated to my mother, Arleney. She is the true queen bee of our family and has taught all of us that there is no such word as *impossible*. Throughout her life she has inspired us with her amazing, uplifting attitude and her positive energy. It is only right that our favorite family holiday, Halloween, should be dedicated to her.

Not-So-Sweet Candy

Something was happening at Samson's house. He was going on so many car rides lately. His family was doing a lot of shopping at lots of different places and coming out with so many bags each time. Mommy took him almost everywhere she went. If it was too hot outside, she made sure that someone stayed in the car with him with the air conditioning on, just so he could go with them in the car. If it was cold, it was cozy and warm in the car, and somebody was always with him. He could not wait for the moment when he was big enough to stick his head out the car window. He tried to do this each time he got in the back seat of the minivan. Today he jumped and jumped, grunting the entire time, but could not reach the window yet. He decided just to sit back and relax and enjoy the warm breeze blowing across his little face and body. He loved his life, and he loved riding in the car.

Normally after a shopping trip, Mom and Dad went into the kitchen to put things away. Samson always hung around, knowing he would get some kind of treat. When things needed to go to the second floor, Mom and Dad would pile up stuff on the stairs and make the kids bring it up. This was great fun for Sammy, who sniffed each bag and ran up and down alongside the kids as they brought the items upstairs. He loved the hustle and bustle of shopping.

Something was different this month. Mom and Dad were buying tons of things and putting everything on the dining room table, instead of in the kitchen or on the stairs. Samson could smell something sweet—some kind of food—and lots of other different smells too. It smelled delicious, and he wanted to get closer for a really good whiff, but every time he did, someone would yell at him to get out of the dining room. This was so unfair and made Samson feel sad. After all, Samson had been allowed to nap in the dining room every day, with the lovely sun coming through the patio doors. All of a sudden, everyone seemed to be allowed in the dining room except him. Mommy was yelling at the kids, telling them not to eat something called "candy" on the table, so Samson guessed that the good-smelling stuff was candy. Maybe he would get his chance to have some. If the kids wanted it that badly, it must be really good.

Those kids were always eating the tastiest things. They were not supposed to give him any human food. Mom and Dad explained over and over that human food was not good for dogs. "How could that be?" Samson wondered. How could anything that smelled so good be so bad for dogs? Sammy had a secret for getting food, though. He would tilt his head to the side and open his eyes really big. Whenever the kids saw his face, they would say, "Aw," and give him a bite or lick of whatever they were eating. This was Sammy's secret look, and the kids could not resist it. Sometimes they got caught giving him handouts, and their parents would yell. But many times they got away with it, and Sammy would just gobble up whatever he could get. Occasionally, he would get stomachaches from the food and would vow not to beg the kids for food again, but he would quickly forget those promises to himself when he smelled their food. And most of the time, his stomach felt just fine. The funny thing is that nobody in the family ever ate his food. He couldn't figure it out. It was delicious, but no humans ever hung around his food bowl wanting to get a taste. He was happy that they all left his food alone. After all, he could not get his own food from the cupboards or the refrigerator. He had to wait for the family to feed him. It was definitely good that they all forgot to eat his food.

Another way that Sammy could eat some human food was to wait for it to drop on the floor. This happened sometimes when Mom was cooking or when food fell out of lunch bags, book bags, or pockets. Sometimes they even left it on the low table in the kitchen. He was able to jump on the bench and get right up there to help himself. Whenever he did this, he got in trouble, but it was mostly worth it. The humans were always so busy that it was like they didn't even think about it. But he was not very busy most days, and food was a big thing to him. His supersmell was always there, reminding him that something scrumptious was waiting for him. He would wait for his opportunity, and when the food fell or was left out, he would run and grab it and take it away to his little blanket before they knew what happened. Sometimes they caught him and took it away, but other times it was too late—Samson gulped it down, and it was gone. Sometimes it did not taste good at first because it had a wrapper on it or it was in some kind of container, but he ate it anyway. Eventually he got to the food. Samson knew one thing for certain: if any of that candy dropped on the floor, he would make sure he was there to sample that sweet-smelling food.

One day his opportunity arrived. All the Parkers had to leave to attend a school event. Samson walked them to the door and was a little upset that they were all leaving him, but today he would finally get to that candy. They shut the front door, and he plodded over to the dining room. To his delight, someone had left a dining-room chair pulled out from the table. He began to climb up the chair. It was so hard. He couldn't seem to make his body tall enough. He really struggled and fell at least ten times. Just as he was about to give up, he landed on the chair. He was face-to-face with bags and boxes of sweet, sweet candy.

Samson just started eating. Everything was wrapped, but he did not care. Everything was so delicious that he could not stop himself. He realized that he could not get the wrappers off, so he just ate them too. He ate and ate and ate. All at once, he realized that he felt awful. His little tummy did not feel good at all. He just wanted to get to his blanket. If he could get there and start to rest, he was sure he would be okay. His little tummy felt like it was going to burst. He looked down at the dining-room chair and panicked. It was a long way down, and he was scared.

He put a paw down to test the distance and fell off the table. Half his body was hanging off the chair, but some of it was still on it. His heart was pounding, but he was able to ease the rest of his body onto the floor. As soon as he got to the floor, he started throwing up. He was gagging and choking, and nobody was home to help him. At the same time, his stomach started to rumble. He had never had that feeling before. He felt like he had to go outside in the yard, which was his toilet. With nobody home to open the door, though, what would he do? He went to the back door, hoping it would open itself. It didn't. Then the most awful thing in the world started to happen—he started going to the bathroom in the house. He went all over the floor near the back door. He felt horrible. Stuff was coming out both ends, and he felt like he was going to die. There was poop and vomit everywhere.

Just then he heard the front door open. He heard Mom say, "What's that awful smell?" She started walking toward the dining room, and her voice started getting really loud. "What the heck? Samson, how did you get to this candy?" The rest of the family joined in with "ew" and "yuck," and everyone had some kind of comment about the smell. If only they knew how horrible he felt. Now he was also ashamed because of the horrible mess he had made in the house.

Mommy did see that he was still hanging around the back door, so she opened it for him, stepping around the puddles of liquid poop. He immediately ran out and was thankful because he was still sick and needed to go more. From outside he could see them all running around with paper towels and bottles of cleaning items. He saw Dad with a mop and pail and all kinds of colorful bottles. He did not want to go back in because he thought they would all be mad at him. Still, those bottles looked like something fun to play with.

After a while, he felt better and went to the back door. Daddy came and opened it for him, but before he would let him in, he bent down to examine him. He picked Sammy up, holding him far away from his body, and announced that Samson smelled really bad, especially his feet. All the kids came running over to get a sniff. Again, they all started shouting "ew" and "yuck" and holding their noses. Daddy announced that Samson would need a bath before he could walk around the house. Daddy carried him up the stairs toward the bathroom, and all the Parkers followed, very excited to hear that they could give Samson his first bath. Sammy didn't know what to think, but he knew that nothing could go wrong if his family was home and taking care of him.

The Crowded Bathroom

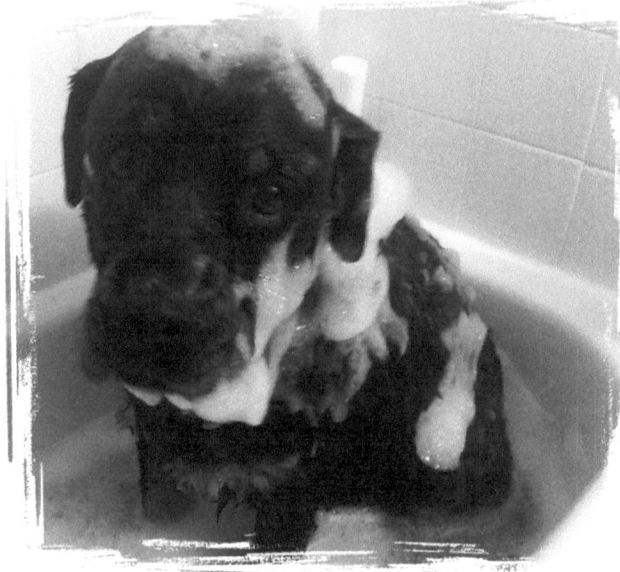

When they got upstairs into the hallway, Mommy and Daddy told the kids what to do. "Linzee, you start running the bathwater, and please do not make it too hot. And put some of that dog shampoo in it to make a few bubbles. Taylor, please get a few towels out of the closet. Someone please run and get the camera." Mommy loved taking pictures more than anyone he knew.

Although everyone could not fit into the bathroom comfortably, they all squished into the small room, sitting on the counter and the toilet and even standing. Everyone watched as Samson got lowered into the water. Daddy started to spread water and bubbles onto Sammy's fur and massage the soapy water all over him. Then the kids screamed that they wanted to give the puppy his first bath. Each kid was finally able to take a few minutes and massage Sammy's soft fur with the bubbles. Samson didn't know what to think, but his tummy felt better now and everyone was fussing over him, which he really enjoyed. The water felt good too. He did try to drink it a few times, but everyone kept yelling at him to stop, so he did. He was getting used to all the yelling in the house. Sometimes it was good yelling, and sometimes it was not good. But he knew they loved each other and him, so it was all good in the end. Finally he was clean, and

Daddy brought Sammy out of the warm water and wrapped a towel around him. Samson felt loved.

One of the kids announced that she was hungry, so everyone headed back to the van to go home. Before they got in, everyone got cleaned off and brushed down. Mom and Dad were always telling the kids that they didn't want the house and car to look like pigsties. Sammy heard the word *pig* and thought back to the time when they went to a petting zoo. There had been a pig there, and they had all been allowed to pet him and stand next to him. He could not understand why Mom and Dad kept talking about that pig. Sammy took a quick peek around before getting into the van, just to see if the pig was there. He didn't see one, so he climbed in with the kids.

When they arrived home, everyone ran to the back of the car to get the bags. Normally, Mom and Dad yelled for the kids to help with bags, but not this time. The kids were back there, grabbing and pushing each other out of the way to get to the bags. Sometimes he didn't understand his humans at all.

The Horrible Machine

Daddy placed Sammy, wrapped in the towel, onto the bathroom counter. He rubbed and massaged Sammy, and it felt wonderful. Just then, Dad asked Mommy to get something called a blow dryer. She reached under the counter to get it—it had a long cord, which she plugged into the wall. Then she turned the switch on. It was so loud that Sammy got nervous again. He started to wiggle and tried to run away. Then the shouting began again. The horrible machine started blowing air all over Sammy. When it got near his eyes, he shut them tight. It was so loud that he could not stand it. He could not relax and kept moving and trying to get away. He swore that he would never eat candy again. This was awful. Mommy told him that if he would just sit still, it would be over faster. He knew that Mommy always knew best, so he froze his body like a statue. Soon the machine was turned off, and the family placed him on the floor; he was finally free. He was so excited that he started dashing from room to room and pushing his face and nose into the carpet. Then he ran really fast past everyone and into the next room and repeated it all again. Everyone was laughing, which made Samson happy, and he kept it up until he was really tired. Life was good again for Samson.

When they all went to sleep that night, he fell immediately asleep because of his exhausting day.

He slept all through the night without waking up. Pretty soon the family's regular weekday

schedules kicked in, and Samson forget about his sick and scary weekend.

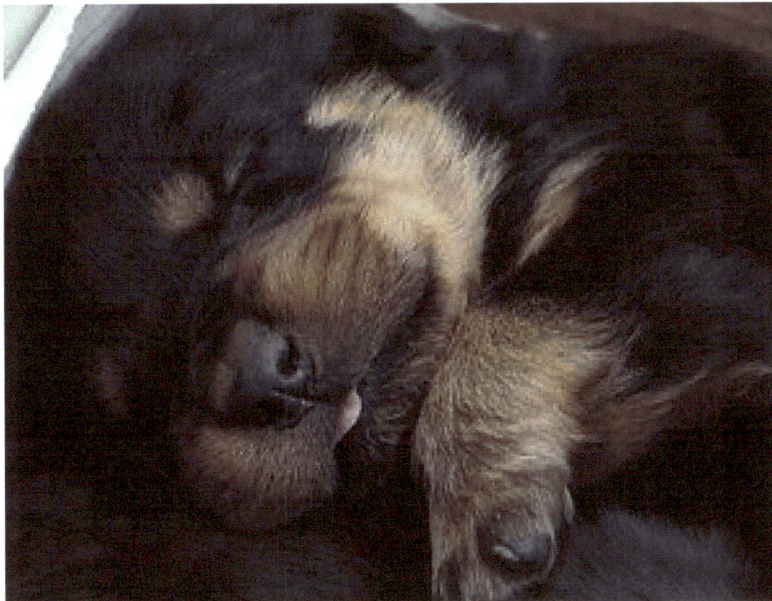

Countdown to Halloween: The Material

Sammy knew that a new weekend was starting. He saw that the sun was shining into the windows instead of the dark, and he didn't get woken up by an alarm clock. He stretched his little paws and yawned. Then he stood up on his back legs and put his front paws on the side of the bed to wake Mommy up. He licked her face until she opened her eyes and started to pet him. He was gently reminding her that it was time for her to get up and take him for a walk. Just like clockwork, Mommy went into the bathroom with her clothes and started to get ready. He stayed to get what the family called "lubby dubbies" from Daddy. This was when Samson would lay on his back and his family would pet his belly and kiss and hug him. It was Sammy's favorite part of the day.

After their walk, Mommy fed him and headed into the living room, drinking a cup of something she called coffee. It smelled just awful, and he was glad she put water into his bowl instead of that stuff. He walked beside her into the living room. She sat on the couch with a little notebook and a pen and began writing things in the book.

One by one, the kids started getting up. When they did, Mommy did something unusual. She made each of them stand up and used what she called a tape measure to get their sizes. She stretched the tape measure around their heads, up their backs, around their waists, and up and around their legs. Then she stopped and wrote a little bit in her notebook. After she was all done, she used the tape measure on Samson too. She announced that they would all be going to a special place that sold something called material. Samson learned by listening that there was a special holiday coming up called Halloween. It involved candy and material. He definitely knew about candy now, but he would learn today about material as well. He was very excited. The kids ate their breakfast and ran upstairs to get dressed.

This time, Daddy went with them but stayed in the car with Samson, who was so curious. He kept staring out the little bit of window he could see out of. Mommy and the kids went into the shop, and it seemed like forever until he saw them again. Eventually, they came out with big bags and put them in the back of the car. Then they jumped into the car, and Samson greeted them like he hadn't seen them for a year. They kept chatting in the car, trying to tell Daddy about the material. It seemed that they had each gotten their own, but mentioned to Dad that they had also gotten some for him and the dog. Samson knew he was "the dog," so he was curious to get home and get his material. He wondered if he could eat it, and he hoped it wouldn't make him as sick as the candy had.

On the way home, the family stopped at a park, and everyone got out to enjoy a nice walk in the beautiful sunshine. There was a sandpit at the park that was always filled with kids and shovels. He tried to run over to it because he had been here many times, digging in the sand, and he loved it. But today there were lots of kids there, so Mommy led him on his leash to the end with no kids in it. He dug in the sand, and it felt so good on his paws.

Some of the kids were pointing and laughing at him, but their parents told them not to go near "that dog." When they said those words, it sounded like a dog was a terrible thing. Samson's heart broke, and he looked sadly at them, wondering why they didn't like him. Just then, Mommy noticed that he was feeling sad. She leaned over to pet his ears and told him what a good boy he was. Mommy always knew how to make him feel better. He kept on digging happily until he was too tired to continue. Then he sat nicely on the sand for a rest in the sun. Mommy was connected to him by his leash, and he felt wonderful.

They went in the front door and brought the bags into the living room. Everyone was shouting again, but they were happy, not mad. They seemed excited as they pulled big sheets of cloth out of the bags. Samson was shocked that these pieces of cloth were causing all this excitement. He learned that this was the material everyone kept mentioning. He could not see how it would be fun.

Soon the material was everywhere. It hung from the couches and was all over the floor, and the kids were twirling around in it. Samson could finally see the fun in it, and he got so excited. He ran around and rolled himself up in it. He began to grip it with his teeth and made his best grumbling and growly noises to show them that he also liked material and was ready to play. To his dismay, everyone started yelling at him, "Sammy, no!" He didn't understand. Didn't they buy this material to have fun? He felt bad and put his head down. But Mommy could see that he only wanted to be part of things, so she pulled some material out of a bag and told Sammy that it was his material. His spirits picked up again, and he raced over to Mommy and grabbed it. His piece of material was so small—it was nothing like the kids' material at all. It would not be any fun to play with. He was very disappointed and could not understand why everyone was so excited. He headed to the kitchen to get some water.

When he came back into the living room, Mommy was kneeling on the floor, unfolding the material. She had a box of pins beside her and a pair of scissors in her hand. He learned what these things were called because just as soon as he stood on the material and tried to sniff everything, his family started yelling again about how he could not stand on the material and how pins and scissors were dangerous. Then they offered to let him go outside in the yard. He was happy.

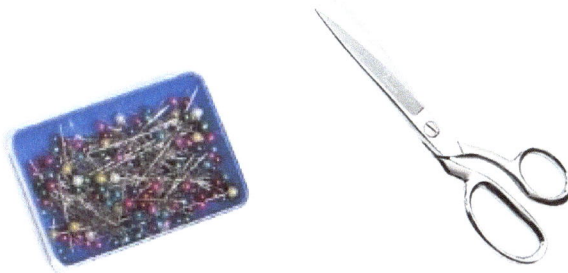

He didn't seem to be doing anything right inside the house today, so he would spend some time outside and enjoy sniffing and watching the neighbors walk by. Some of the neighbors called out, "Hi, Sam." He loved that. Others walked by, and some pointed at him and said things like, "Is that a Rottweiler?" It didn't sound like being a Rottweiler was a good thing. He heard that often, and it made him feel sad, just as he had at the park today. How could people not like you when they didn't know you? He was enjoying his yard though, and his family was inside. He soon forgot about it because he knew his family loved him, and that was all that mattered.

Mommy Sewed All Day

Sammy heard some noise coming from inside the house. He could see Daddy lifting something onto the table. Mommy was sitting in a chair next to the table. She had a huge piece of material in her hands and was leaning over whatever Daddy had put on the table. Samson just had to see what was going on. He walked to the back door and scratched at the door. Mommy turned around and opened the door to let him in. Once she sat back down, she leaned on a machine of some sort. She clicked a button, and the machine started making a very loud noise. This scared Samson, and he ran across the room as fast as he could. He bumped into Linzee. She bent down and asked him if he was scared of the sewing machine. He frantically started licking her and jumping on her legs, begging to be picked up.

Linzee sat on the couch and picked him up and put him in her lap. She petted him and soothed him. It worked for a while, but that noise was still too scary for Samson. He left Linzee and ran up the stairs. He lay down in his little bed, where it was nice and quiet. He could still hear that Mommy was using the machine downstairs, but it wasn't as loud upstairs. He would stay here until she was done. He fell asleep waiting.

Later that day he heard the family running around and calling his name. They seemed upset. He got up and went to the top of the stairs. His family was standing at the bottom, looking up at him. He was still sleepy, but he could tell they were really happy to see him. It was as if they hadn't known where he was. They were all saying, "Whew, he's in the house after all." Sammy knew then that his family had lost track of him because he had been upstairs alone all day. It felt really good to know they loved him so much. And his tummy was growling too. He knew it was dinnertime. Mommy had been at that stupid sewing machine all day. But finally that awful noise stopped, and she was in the kitchen making dinner and wonderful smells. The family took some time to eat dinner. Then Mommy and Daddy cleaned the kitchen, while the kids went into the living room to play with him.

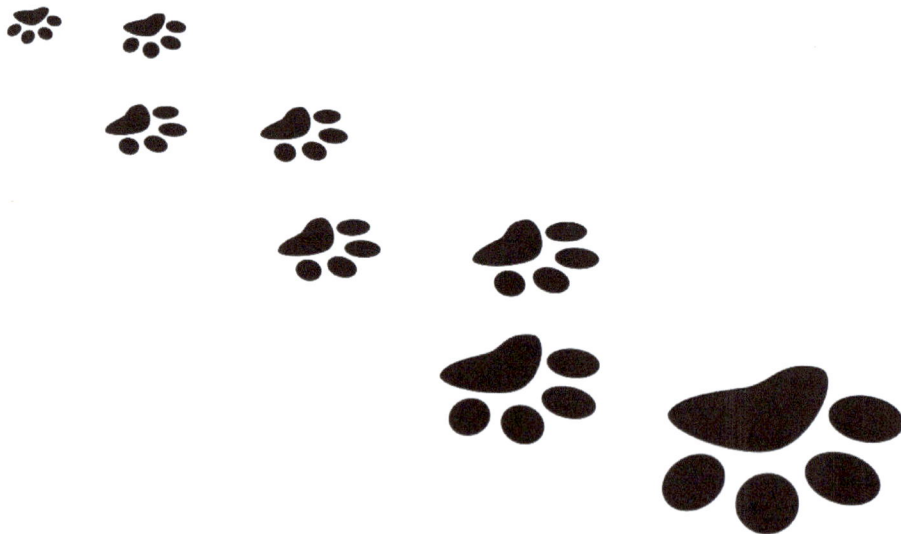

Masks, Costumes, and Makeup

Mommy started passing out clothes to the kids and asking them to try them on. The clothes looked exactly like the material she had been sewing earlier. Samson put two and two together and realized that Mommy had been making clothes for the kids. But the clothes looked strange—not like the normal clothes the kids wore. The clothes were dark, and the kids were wearing hats and hoods and looked a little scary. Sammy was glad he knew them all because if he hadn't, he would have been afraid.

All of a sudden, Daddy asked if they had bought something called masks. The kids ran to the shopping bags and started pulling more items out of the bags. The kids put masks on their faces. They also ran to the mirrors to see how they looked. Samson was terrified. He didn't recognize anyone and could not tell one kid from the other. They had these scary faces now, and they were running around making scary noises and walking slowly with their hands up in the air, claiming to be something called zombies. What in the world was happening at Samson's house?

Sammy ran into the kitchen to get comfort from Daddy, but when he saw Daddy, he was more scared than ever. Daddy also had a very scary mask on. He was talking to Samson, but it sounded muffled and not like Daddy's normal, nice voice. Samson didn't feel safe in there either.

Sammy ran up the stairs as fast as his legs could go. He would get right back in his little bed, and he would be safe there. He would go right to sleep, hoping that when he woke up, it would all just be a dream and his family would look normal again.

The kids and Daddy felt bad—they had never meant to scare Sammy. They took off their masks and went up to the bedroom to talk to him and make sure he was okay. They coaxed him out of his bed and tried to make him feel better. Then they asked him to come downstairs for treats. Whew, it was all over. Treats and his family—things were back to normal, thank goodness.

After Samson ate his treats, his family brought him into the living room. They told him not to be scared, and they sat down on the floor with their masks. They didn't put them on their faces this time; instead, they held the masks in their hands and let Sammy sniff and lick them. Samson completely relaxed. They were just plastic. They could not hurt him. He was no longer afraid.

Linzee went into the kitchen. She called Sammy in and told him she had a mask for him. He loved when Linzee fussed over him, but he did not want this mask on. He did not want to wear anything that had to do with Halloween.

Busy Daddy

Another week went by, and once again it was the weekend. This time Samson woke up, but Daddy and Mommy got up first. They got dressed and ready and scratched Samson's body and ears. He loved mornings with his Mommy and Daddy. All three of them went downstairs. Dad headed to the door to let Sammy out to do his morning business. Mommy headed to the kitchen to prepare drinks and food for everyone. Sammy ran back to the door and scratched on it when he realized that food was being made in the kitchen. When he came into the kitchen, he saw that his food and water bowl had been filled up with food and fresh, cool water. He began eating, and Mommy promised that they would have their walk later.

🐾

Soon Daddy got up and stretched and said, "Guess we better get to it." Sammy had no idea what he meant, but Daddy headed to the closet nearest the kitchen, opened the door, and pulled out a huge piece of wood. When the wood came out, Sammy got scared and jumped. Daddy yelled at him to move out of the way so he didn't get hurt. Samson backed up a little but wanted to keep his eye on what was happening.

Daddy went down into a hole in the floor of the closet. Samson was shocked! He ran over to the hole and saw the top of Daddy's head. What was that place? Daddy called for Mommy to come and help. Daddy started handing scary-looking things to Mommy out of that hole. She took them from him and placed them on the kitchen floor. Yikes! Samson had no idea what was going on now. There were weird-looking plastic things with terrible faces. Sammy was scared again. He kept thinking back to the weekend before with the material and the masks and also to the week before that and the candy incident. Was this how his life would be? Every weekend he would be scared to death living in his own house?

Painting with Taylor

The same day that Daddy was taking decorations out of the basement, Taylor was painting pumpkins in the backyard. She had her dishes full of paint and her water ready. She also had an array of paintbrushes waiting to be used. Taylor didn't want any of the other kids around. They kept making fun of her because she was the smallest one, and they said her pumpkins were ugly. She wanted to be left alone to paint her pumpkins and surprise the rest of the family. She knew her pumpkins were beautiful, and she didn't care what any of them thought. So she settled into the backyard for her creative project. She needed some peace and quiet to create her works of art.

Since Samson was getting under everyone's feet while they were trying to decorate, everyone decided he should go into the yard with Taylor. At first Taylor thought this was a great idea. Sammy loved hearing her chatter on and on about Halloween and her paints and the pumpkins and how good they would look for Halloween. But when Samson tried to get involved by drinking the water and licking the paint, Taylor got mad at him. She knew he wouldn't get hurt because the paint was nontoxic, but he was crawling all over her, trying to show her that he loved paint too. She went through several different outfits, running in and out to change, because Samson wouldn't stop getting into her paint and crawling on her. She kept crying to Mommy and Daddy, but they insisted that the yard was the only place Samson was safe and out of everyone's hair.

Finally, despite Samson's interference, Taylor finished her pumpkins. She was horrified to see Samson painted every color she had in the yard. She knew that everyone would be really mad at her if she let the dog into the house with paint all over him, even if it was washable. She got the brilliant idea to use the hose on him and herself to wash the paint off. When she started squirting, Sammy started barking and growling at the hose. He was having the time of his life, and Taylor was having fun playing with him. They were both drenched, but it was a warm day, so she didn't feel too cold.

Soon Mommy came around the back fence to tell Taylor something. Mommy was surprised that the yard was such a mess, and there was paint and water everywhere. But she laughed when she saw Taylor and Samson. She handed Taylor the leash and told her that the decorations were done in front. She asked Taylor to bring Samson to the front of the house so they could see the decorations.

Sammy started panting and jumping. He realized that he had missed seeing his mommy all day. He ran out the back gate with Taylor trailing behind.

Spooky Can Be Good

When they got to the front of the house, Sammy stopped and stared. He could not believe it. The decorations from inside the house were now outside the house. Daddy had arranged them nicely all across the front of the house. Some of the decorations played music and talked. Some of them also moved. Samson was frightened. He tried to run away from Taylor, but she had a tight grip on his leash and told him no. He wanted to be a good boy and listen, so he didn't move a muscle. Plus, Daddy was there on the front lawn, taking pictures and being his silly self. He liked that about Daddy. If Daddy liked the decorations and wasn't afraid, he certainly wouldn't let anything happen to Samson.

Daddy told the kids to take Samson around to all the decorations and show him that there was nothing to be afraid of, just as they had done with the masks. Once Samson realized that the decorations were not going to hurt him in any way, he began to relax.

Mommy and Daddy asked everyone to clean up the bags and boxes the decorations had been packed in. Mommy said she would take Samson for a nice walk and come home and cook dinner for the family. Daddy had a twinkle in his eye when he told the kids they would all come out and look at the decorations once it got dark. He promised them that the decorations would look very spooky.

After dinner was over, the family went outside to look at the decorations. They shut the door behind them and brought the camera to take pictures. Sammy knew they were happy because once again they were shouting in a very happy, excited way. Sure enough, the decorations looked even better in the dark. They were ready for Halloween the next weekend.

Throughout the week, people who lived close by stopped over to see the house and the decorations. They also drove by at night to see them all lit up. The kids and Mommy and Daddy were all getting excited about the upcoming holiday.

Halloween Is the Best Holiday After All

Finally, the big night arrived—it was Halloween. You could feel the excitement in the air. The house started getting loud and busy immediately after the kids arrived home from school. Linzee cuddled Samson, telling him that tonight would be really fun and that he should not worry.

The kids ran all over, looking for their masks and costumes. They had plans to visit all the houses in the neighborhood and get candy (yuck). The kids in the neighborhood would also come to their house for candy. Daddy would take the kids trick-or-treating, while Mommy stayed home to give candy away.

Daddy put Samson on his leash and told him that he would have a fun walk through the neighborhood, but not to be scared of the costumes and masks. Samson had a very good time and waited politely with Daddy at the end of each sidewalk while the kids got their candy. Everyone in the neighborhood looked like they were having fun.

But some kids walked by Samson and started screaming. He wasn't doing a thing. He was just walking by Daddy's side and quietly sitting down at each house. What was wrong with them? He didn't even have his mask or costume on. He couldn't walk properly in them, so his family decided to leave them home. The kids were pointing at him again and acting like they were afraid. It made Sammy feel so bad. All those kids and their parents were running through the neighborhood dressed as monsters and zombies and all kinds of scary things. Their faces were painted, their masks were scary, and still they were pointing and screaming at *him*. If anyone should be afraid, it should be Samson. But his family had taught him that costumes and makeup were not real. The people underneath them were real, and he should not be afraid of or judge people for how they looked on the outside.

Samson learned many valuable lessons that Halloween season. He would never again be afraid of costumes or material. At various times throughout his life though, especially at Halloween, he tried a little bit of candy. As he grew, he realized that a tiny bit of candy did not make him sick, but never again did he gobble it up, especially with all the wrappers on it. Mommy and Daddy were right—his dog treats tasted much better, and he actually preferred them.

Samson continued to walk around the neighborhood each year on Halloween with Daddy, Mommy, or the kids. People got used to seeing him, and some of the moms and dads were even happy to see that he was there to watch over their children. There were always some people who didn't like him just because of the way he looked, but they missed out on knowing that Samson loved them all. They just did not understand. You must give love to get love. Samson was so glad to be a Parker and to have learned that.

Every year Samson knew it was time for Halloween when all the shopping started. He got excited when it came time for putting candy on the dining-room table, shopping for material, decorating, and painting the pumpkins. He realized it was traditions like these that bonded his family together. There was nothing quite as fun as Halloween at Samson Parker's house.

From the Authors

We sincerely hope that you enjoyed *Halloween at Samson Parker's House*. We hope you will keep checking our website for all our Samson Parker books. If you haven't read the very first Samson Parker book, *Samson Parker Gets a New Home*, you can go to www.amazon.com and search for "Samson Parker." When Sammy goes home with his new family and becomes a Parker, it will melt your heart.

Visit the following website for more information about the Parkers and all their dogs and for general information on Rottweilers: www.rottweilertales.com.

Samson Parker also has his own Facebook Page (Samson Parker)!

Monthly Prize Giveaway

www.rottweilertales.com/contest.html

Once a month, one lucky winner will be randomly selected to receive a Samson Parker plush toy. Please go to the contest link above and fill out the brief survey and a plush Rottweiler could be on its way to you!

Please allow four to six weeks for delivery.

For each book purchased, one dollar will automatically be donated to the Northeast Rottweiler

Rescue: http://www.rottrescue.org/

Rottweiler Facts

For a full list of facts, please visit us at http://www.rottweilertales.com/rottweilertales.html.

Never get *any* dog if it is not going to be a part of your family. People get Rottweilers and do not realize how large and boisterous they will get—and the solution too often is to put them outside. Rotties don't like to be on chains outside your homes, looking in, watching their humans having fun without them. Each moment you leave your Rottweiler, you break its heart. Remember that while you have a full life, they only have *you*.

Owning a Rottweiler is a huge commitment. Because they are such a smart breed, they tend to take over in a family as "alpha" if not trained properly. You must commit to daily training for your Rottweiler's lifetime. Puppies are loads of work with any breed, but Rotties are very smart and will try to be in charge whenever possible. You need to let this breed know who is boss.

This breed needs to be exercised on a daily basis because they are lazy by nature and will enjoy just lying around and eating. The leaner you can keep your Rottie, the longer his or her life-span will be. The exercise will be good for both of you.

You should never approach a dog without asking the owner if it is okay to pet that dog. And you should never allow strangers to approach your dog unless you are there to hold the dog and assure him or her that everything is fine.

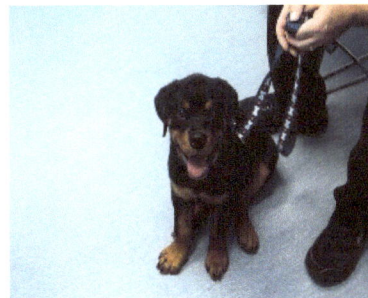

Some people think that Rottweilers are nasty by nature, and as a result, Rotties get a bad reputation. Rottweilers are just like any animal. If you treat them kindly, they will respond with kindness. If you are mean to them, they will be forced to go on the defensive. Because Rotties are dogs that will weigh over fifty pounds, they can do more damage than smaller breeds. Therefore, if your Rottweiler is not well trained, you have a potential weapon on your hands.

Rottweilers are clowns and love to be the center of attention. They need love and playtime with their humans. While it is difficult to ignore the equivalent of a baby horse running around your house, sometimes people get mad when they get stepped on or pushed over. This is the human's responsibility. It boils down to training. Don't allow your Rottweiler to jump. Don't play tug-of-war games with your Rottweiler. If you put your Rottie in a position where it can win or lose, it will most certainly want to win. People, especially small ones, can get hurt because this breed is so large.

Rottweilers love to push their rear ends into you and lean on you if they love you. They also tend to step on your feet. Please wear slippers or shoes in your house when playing with your Rottie.

Please visit us at www.rottweilertales.com to keep up with the progress of all our books.